CAMPING WITH PUP

BY **ANDREW CAPSTICK**
ILLUSTRATED BY **ROBERT SNYDER**

Scott Foresman
is an imprint of

Glenview, Illinois • Boston, Massachusetts • Mesa, Arizona
Shoreview, Minnesota • Upper Saddle River, New Jersey

Photographs

Every effort has been made to secure permission and provide appropriate credit for photographic material. The publisher deeply regrets any omission and pledges to correct errors called to its attention in subsequent editions.

Unless otherwise acknowledged, all photographs are the property of Pearson Education, Inc.

Photo locators denoted as follows: Top (T), Center (C), Bottom (B), Left (L), Right (R), Background (Bkgd)

8 Comstock/Thinkstock.

Illustrations Robert Snyder.

ISBN 13: 978-0-328-39356-5
ISBN 10:   0-328-39356-8

Copyright © Pearson Education, Inc. or its affiliate(s). All Rights Reserved.
Printed in the United States of America. This publication is protected by copyright and permission should be obtained from the publisher prior to any prohibited reproduction, storage in a retrieval system, or transmission in any form or by any means, electronic, mechanical, photocopying, recording, or otherwise. For information regarding permission(s), write to: Pearson School Rights and Permissions, One Lake Street, Upper Saddle River, New Jersey 07458.

Pearson and Scott Foresman are trademarks, in the U.S. and/or other countries, of Pearson Education, Inc. or its affiliate(s).

10 V010 17 16 15 14 13

Pup is camping with Mother and Father. It is a beautiful place. He couldn't be happier.

"I would love to build a fire,"
Pup said. "Please show me how."
   "You are too small to build a fire,"
Mother said. "But you can help."

"I would love to put up a tent,"
Pup said. "Please show me how."
   "You are too small to put it up
straight," Father said. "But you can help."

"I would love to scare a bear!"
Pup said.

"We don't need to scare a bear.
We need some fish," said Father.

They fished at the stream. "After supper, you need to sleep," said Mother.

"I will! Camping makes me sleepy," Pup said.

Learning About the Land

Read Together

Did you notice that Pup camped in the mountains? Did you notice that Pup camped by a stream?

Camping is a great way to learn about the land. You can camp on a mountain, in a valley, or in the desert. Many campers choose campsites near the water. You can camp near a river, a pond, a lake, or an ocean.